I LIVE IN AMERICA

I LIVE IN AMERICA

AN ILLUSTRATED TOUR OF AMERICA

Written and Illustrated by

ELIZABETH NELSON

with ROBERT NELSON

GREENWICH PRESS

DENVER

Nelson, Elizabeth, 1938-
    I Live In America : an illustrated tour of America / written and illustrated by Elizabeth Nelson
with Robert Nelson. -- 1st ed.
    p.   cm. -- (I live in--)
    SUMMARY: Illustrations and background texts take readers on a journey to places and events
that express what it is like to live in America.
    LCCN: 2003110261
    ISBN: 0-9714078-1-9

    1. United States--Description and travel--Juvenile literature. 2. Historic buildings--United
States--Juvenile literature. 3. Art, American--United States--Juvenile literature. [1. United States--
Description and travel. 2. Historic buildings. 3. Art, American] I. Title.

E169.04N45 2004   973
                                QBI03-700460

Printed and Bound in the United States of America
by
Colorado Printing Company
Grand Junction, Colorado
and
Roswell Bookbinding
Phoenix, Arizona

Acknowledgement

From the inception of "I Live In America," it was our dream to have the book produced, printed and bound in the United States. For the production work, we would like to acknowledge the efforts of Scott O'Neil of Reed Photo-Imaging in Denver, Colorado for his tireless efforts to achieve the best color reproduction of the artwork. We would also like to thank Mike Antonucci of Colorado Printing in Grand Junction, Colorado for making our dream of printing "I Live In America" in the United States a reality; his competitive spirit and creative imagination represents what's best in American business. Finally, we would like to thank Roswell Bookbinding of Phoenix, Arizona for being a part of our team.

Dedication

We dedicate this book to the memory of our parents. Elizabeth's mother, Harriet Zaremba Haeger, came to America from Poland in 1913 and Bob's father, Gunnerd Nelson, arrived from Sweden in 1917. Their courage and spirit of adventure represents the journey of many of the people who formed this great country.

Prologue

    "I Live In America" is the second book in a series. It was influenced by the authors' parents who both emigrated from Europe in the early 1900s – Elizabeth's mother from Poland and Bob's father from Sweden. Both of them came into America through Ellis Island and eventually settled in Chicago. The authors have either lived in or visited all of the places portrayed in Elizabeth's paintings, but the collection also represents the journeys taken by millions of immigrants and later-generation offspring who settled in parts of the country that reminded them of their homelands. These paintings also offer an overview of what has happened in the past to make America great, as well as what sustains us today.

Americans are a nation of travelers and movers. We are probably the most mobile society in recorded history and we are fortunate, indeed, to have many opportunities to relocate, as well as to have so many beautiful and exciting places to visit and live. In this book, we have tried to provide not just an overview of places that represent America, but also individuals and events that are typically American. Because of the sheer size and diversity of our country, we were not able to portray every state and every major city, but we hope that we have presented a reasonable cross-section that everyone can appreciate. Hopefully, some of your favorite places and American institutions have been included. It is our goal that this book illustrates some of the history of our nation and a sense of why America is a source of pride and inspiration to all. Even today, our country is a beacon of hope for new immigrants from around the world who continue to come to our beautiful country and begin new lives.

Those of you who read Elizabeth's first book, "I Live In Denver," know that our Old English Sheepdog, Alfie, was your guide in visiting Denver and was located somewhere in each of the paintings. A short time ago, Alfie passed on but he's still here in spirit, so look for him in each of the paintings in "I Live In America" – he's there if you look carefully!

Elizabeth and Bob Nelson

July, 2003

TABLE OF CONTENTS

Arriving at Ellis Island
from countries across the sea,

Coming to America,
seeking opportunity

in the Land of the Free.

Ellis Island and The Statue of Liberty – Coming to America

Imagine coming to America from Poland in 1913 with all you own in two suitcases, spending eight days in the cramped steerage compartment of a small ship with hundreds of other people. Suddenly, someone shouts that they can see land! You first see the Statue of Liberty and are joyful. Then, you see the buildings of Ellis Island, where you will be processed after docking in New York City; your feelings turn more somber. Those in first and second class are released at the docks after brief inspections; you take a shuttle to Ellis Island. After interrogation and a brief medical inspection you are cleared to get a rail ticket to somewhere in America or a ferry back to the city. If your family meets you, they might take you to a public restroom where they dress you in American clothes so no one thinks you are a greenhorn "just off the boat!" Roughly one in six are held with their families for several days. If the doctor puts a chalk mark on your coat for some suspected problem (e.g., 'L'-lame, 'F'-facial rash) you have to remain for a more detailed medical inspection. Only 2% are deported back to Europe. It's chaotic (as many as 15,000 people are processed per day), the food is terrible (prunes and bread served on dirty plates) and you may lose half of your money or more in currency exchange and purchasing a rail ticket. Still, your future is bright, for you have arrived in the land of freedom and opportunity!

The Statue of Liberty, located on Bedloe's Island (renamed Liberty Island in 1956), was dedicated on October 28, 1886. It was a gift from the French people honoring America's independence from Great Britain. Standing 150 feet tall (305 feet including the pedestal), it was designed by the French sculptor Auguste Bartholdi and the internal support system was constructed by Gustave Eiffel, the engineer who built the Eiffel Tower. Edouard de Laboulaye is known as the Father of the Statue of Liberty; he single-handedly raised 400,000 francs ($250,000) for its design and construction but did not live to see his project realized, as he died in 1883. Restorations in 1937-39 and 1982-86 dealt with heavy corrosion and structural updates to keep Lady Liberty in good shape.

From 1892 through 1954, approximately 15 million immigrants entered America through Ellis Island. Today, over 100 million Americans are descended from these brave people who gave up all they had to pursue a dream in a faraway land. It is now a part of the Statue of Liberty-Ellis Island National Monument and is visited by over one million people per year. The Ellis Island Immigrant Museum contains an Oral History Studio and an American Immigrant Wall of Honor that holds the names of more than 200,000 immigrants. Some bought rail tickets and fanned out to all parts of America; others stayed where they landed and formed the vibrant, multi-cultural community we know as New York City.

Having fun after dark
In New York City's
Central Park.

12

New York City – Central Park

For those immigrants who settled in New York City, Central Park was a beautiful green jewel set in the middle of a huge concrete jungle. By the time of the Great Migration of over 10 million immigrants between 1900 and 1914, Central Park had been built in the city using the English pastoral style of Hyde Park in London. Prior to its creation, there were no parks in the city. Then, in 1853, the state set aside 843 acres of rocky, muddy land in the middle of the city for such a purpose. Considered unsuitable for commercial use, it ultimately became home to over 300,000 trees and shrubs after tons of dirt, gravel and sand had been hauled in for landscaping. It also includes four lakes and many bridges and footpaths. Designed by Frederick Law Olmstead and Calvert Vaux, it was completed in 1877. The Greensward Plan, the master design, was designed to insulate the park from the surrounding city and create a feeling of being in a natural setting. Central Park was originally intended as a nature preserve primarily for the wealthy, with wide roads for afternoon carriage rides. Over the years, more and more "common people" came to use it as public transportation improved and playgrounds and ball fields were added. Originally, it had only four buildings, among them the Dairy. It was used to dispense milk to a needy public during a time when tainted milk was a public-health hazard due to the dairy cows being fed brewery mash instead of hay! The Dairy is now a Visitors Center for the park.

Today, Central Park includes several museums, a zoo, a carousel and the Tavern on the Green, a world-class restaurant that was originally a sheepfold until 1934, when grazing sheep were removed from what is now the Sheep Meadow. At one time, the Casino restaurant sold beer for five cents a glass, but in 1925 it became embroiled in scandal under Mayor Jimmy Walker when he used city park funds to make it his personal club. It was later torn down and turned into a playground. Over the years, many statues have been erected, including the popular Alice in Wonderland and Balto the rescue dog.

Central Park has had a colorful history of "boom and bust," with periods of repair and expansion followed by budget cuts that allowed it to deteriorate and lose much of its charm. It was first a political football between the state and the city and it later became a part of New York City politics under several mayors. However, it always survived because it was valued so much by the people of New York City as a haven and a place of recreation. From The Ramble, a six-acre wild garden that is a bird-watcher's paradise, to the Great Lawn and Sheep Meadow where thousands gather regularly, it offers something for everyone. Known as "the lungs of the city," Central Park's importance is perhaps best represented by the times in the 1960s when Mayor John Lindsay created a program called "Fun City," bringing in many young people and minorities for dance parties and kite-flying contests. It is now supported largely by private funding through the Central Park Conservancy which, over the last 25 years, has not only refurbished and maintained the Park but has also upgraded it with even more playgrounds and ball fields. Whether for a gathering of 10,000 or two solitary skaters, Central Park has provided recreation for everyone who lives in New York City. In 2003, this beautiful jewel celebrated its 150th year with a number of gala celebrations – Happy Anniversary, Central Park!

Our nation's Capitol
on the Fourth of July;
a celebration of independence
with fire in the sky.

The Capitol Building on the 4th of July

The Capitol Building is the seat of our national government, housing both the Senate and the House of Representatives in its 16 acres of floor space and 540 rooms. It has a colorful history that closely parallels that of Washington, D.C., our nation's capital city.

The Capitol's story begins in the very early days of our country, shortly after our Declaration of Independence from Great Britain on July 4, 1776, the Revolutionary War being won in 1783 and the Constitution having been written in 1787. New York City was the nation's capital, but the decision was made to move to another city. Philadelphia was favored, but Thomas Jefferson and Alexander Hamilton met over dinner in New York City and reached a compromise to establish a new capital in the South so the surrounding states would pay off their war debts. Maryland and Virginia donated about 100 square miles of land near the Potomac River. In 1790, Congress passed the Residence Act and named the new capital Washington, in honor of our first president. President Washington appointed a French city planner, Pierre Charles L'Enfant, to design the city and its major buildings. L'Enfant was fired after only one year, but the basics of his city design have lasted until this day thanks to Benjamin Banneker, a free black farmer and self-taught surveyor. Because L'Enfant had taken all of the plans with him when he stormed off the job, Banneker laid out the city plan from memory, as he had worked with L'Enfant.

A competition was held for a design of the Capitol Building and in 1792 a British West Indies doctor and amateur architect, William Thornton, was chosen as the winner. In 1793, Washington laid the cornerstone for the 'Federal House' (later to be renamed the Capitol Building). It was built on Jenkins

Hill, called by L'Enfant "a pedestal waiting for a monument." Surviving a series of architects, lack of funding and being burned during the War of 1812, the Capitol Building was finally completed after 37 years, in 1826. As the country grew and expanded, so also the Capitol Building was enlarged, first in 1851. It was then remodeled during the Civil War, when a two-piece cast-iron dome weighing 4,500 tons replaced the old wooden dome. The dome is over the Rotunda, where past presidents have been laid in state upon their deaths. The Rotunda separates the House Chamber in the South Wing and the Senate Chamber in the North Wing. With its own power plant, post office, subway system, barber shops and banks, the Capitol is a self-contained small city, an architectural jewel that sits opposite the White House (first called the "President's Palace"). The two buildings are 1.8 miles apart on either end of Pennsylvania Avenue.

On July 4th each year, we celebrate Independence Day. In Washington, D.C., the celebration begins with the National Independence Day Parade down Constitution Avenue, including floats, beauty queens and marching bands from all around the country. There is a Revolutionary War campsite set up near the National Archives building and men and women read the Declaration of Independence to the crowds. The festivities are completed with an outdoor concert and, as shown, a spectacular fireworks display on the National Mall near the Capitol Building. Happy Birthday, America!

North Carolina's Outer Banks,
birthplace of flight;
playground of sun, sand and sea,
an American delight.

North Carolina's Outer Banks – America's Majestic Sea Shore

The next stop on our tour of America is North Carolina and its Outer Banks. One of the original 13 colonies, North Carolina was the site of an early colony of British settlers at Roanoke Island in 1587 and it was here that the first British baby, Virginia Dare, was born in North America. Roanoke Island was called the "Lost Colony" because its residents disappeared and were believed to have been absorbed into the surrounding Indian cultures. Indeed, some Lumbee Indians still living in the area have blue eyes and blond hair.

There are three major sections of North Carolina, ranging from the Great Smoky and Blue Ridge Mountains, to the Piedmont region of rolling hills and farm land, to the Atlantic Coastal Plain, an area of swamps and low-lying land near the Atlantic Ocean. North Carolina is a folksy, charming state that is known for artist colonies and many festivals. For example, the National Hollerin' Contest hearkens back to the days when farmers communicated by shouting across their fields and is held in Spivey's Corner in late June. The Ole-Time Fiddler's and Blue Grass Festival takes place in Union Grove on the last weekend in May. Gold was discovered in Little Meadow Creek near Charlotte in 1799, sparking America's first gold rush.

The Outer Banks is a long line of sandbars that spans most of North Carolina's 301 miles of coastline. A dreamy, beautiful area, the Outer Banks stand about 12 feet high and range in width from about 3,000 feet to three miles. The pure, white beaches and grassy dunes are a haven for summer homes and visitors from all over the country. The steady winds make it ideal for kite flying and it was here, 100 years ago, that the Wright Brothers flew their "motorized flying machine" off an 80-foot ramp in the Kill Devil Hill dunes for 12 seconds, traveling all of 120 feet. This took place on December 17, 1903 at Kitty Hawk and it marks the beginning of manned flight. It's inspiring to think about how this modest beginning has been transformed into supersonic jet planes and space shuttles in less than a century's time!

The history of the Outer Banks is colorful and exciting. The channels and coastal swamps were hiding places for Blackbeard and other pirates who hid in lairs such as Ocracoke Island and raided commercial European ships coming into the colonies. Blackbeard was killed in 1718 by an English navy lieutenant, Robert Maynard, who brought the pirate's severed head back to port to prove that he was dead. The Cape Hatteras lighthouse, 208 feet high and built in 1870, was moved 2,900 feet inland in 1999 to protect it from the encroaching ocean that threatened to wash it away. For ships, this area is known as the "Graveyard of the Atlantic" due to the shifting sands and fierce weather. The Cape Hatteras National Sea Shore, established in 1953, preserves this area which, at 72 miles, is the longest beach on the East Coast.

The Outer Banks are a magical place that are a treat to visit, with dolphins and whales frolicking in the ocean and wild ponies roaming Assateague Island. There is an old graveyard in Beaufort on the mainland that has headstones dating back to the early 1700s. If you happen to get caught there at night, you might be surprised by seeing Blackbeard's ghost or Robert Maynard waving his severed head in the foggy, misty night air!

23

Chicago and its Magnificent Mile; America's Midwestern city with world-class style.

Chicago – The Windy City

Chicago grew up as a blue-collar city in the Midwest, but it has developed into a world-class center of culture and entertainment. It has survived devastating fires, political turmoil and a reputation as a haven for gangsters to become what it is today – one of the finest cities in America. For many thousands of years it was home to the Potawatami Indians, who named it Chicago, a "wild onion place." In 1779, Jean Baptiste Point DuSable, a black Haitian trader, was the first settler, on the north bank of the Chicago River near Lake Michigan. In 1804, Fort Dearborn was built on the same site, but it was destroyed by fire in 1812 in the Fort Dearborn Massacre. In 1833, Chicago became a chartered city, with 350 residents.

The city grew rapidly, with wood being used for many buildings, sidewalks and even street pavement. On October 8, 1871 the Great Chicago Fire destroyed most of the city, taking 300 lives, leaving 100,000 homeless and creating $200 million in property losses. Popular legend has it that the fire was started when Mrs. O'Leary's cow kicked over a kerosene lamp in the milking shed, but this was never proven. In true Chicago fashion, this disaster was taken as an opportunity to rebuild the city from scratch; architects poured in to work on this "blank canvas." It was here that the modern skyscraper was born in 1884, in the form of the ten-story Home Insurance Building. It was made possible by the developments of steel framing and the elevator; William Le Baron Jenney designed it and created the "Chicago School" of architecture.

In 1893, the World's Fair was held in Chicago and a second one took place there in 1933 for the city's centennial celebration. The 1893 Fair had 27 million visitors and featured the first Ferris wheel. A large demonstration of electricity and the white plaster on many of the buildings gave it the nickname "White City." The nickname most often associated with Chicago is "The Windy City", due to the strong winds that blow into the city off Lake Michigan.

In the early 1900s, immigrants flocked to Chicago and created ethnic neighborhoods in different parts of the city – Germans, Poles and Scandinavians on the North Side, African Americans on the South Side, and Italians, Slavs, Greeks and Jews on the West Side. Chicago has the second-largest Polish population in the world after Warsaw. Chicago is also a city of 542 parks covering some 7,500 acres and large nature sanctuaries just outside the city, called Forest Preserves. The largest park in the city is Lincoln Park, which includes a zoo, two beaches and Belmont Harbor, shown in the painting. Nearby is Michigan Avenue, Chicago's "Magnificent Mile" along the Lakefront. Other aspects of Chicago's colorful past and present include the development of blues and jazz music; gangster times in the 1920s and 1930s featuring such characters as Al Capone and John Dillinger; and the development of the atom bomb at the University of Chicago in 1942.

Chicago holds a special place in the authors' hearts, as both their parents were married there and both were born there. While it is now a modern, sophisticated city, it retains the image best described in Carl Sandburg's poem, "Chicago:"

"Hog butcher to the world,
Tool maker, stacker of wheat,
Player with the nation's railroads and nation's freight handlers,
Stormy, husky, brawling,
City of the big shoulders…"

Main Street America,

Route 66;

pop-art attractions,

a unique American mix.

Route 66 – Main Street America

Since Henry Ford made gasoline-powered automobiles available to millions, America has been a country on wheels. During the 1940s, '50s and '60s, many Americans' vacations were road trips on the nation's highways. One of the longest and most memorable was along Route 66 from Chicago to Santa Monica, California, a journey of 2,297 miles. In those days, the roads weren't that great and cars weren't as fast as they are now, so even a two-week vacation couldn't cover the entire highway, which was immortalized by John Steinbeck in his novel "The Grapes of Wrath" as "The Mother Road." It was also called "America's Worst Speed Trap" and "Main Street America" because it ran through the middle of many towns and cities before it was largely replaced by the Interstate Highway System. Officially, Route 66 is no longer a Federal Highway, but parts of it still exist as state highways and it lives on in the hearts and minds of millions of Americans who traveled its colorful pavement.

Route 66's official beginning was in 1925 when it was designated as the western half of what had been the coast-to-coast Lincoln Highway. Its creator, Cyrus Avery, succeeded in creating a southern route going through downstate Illinois, Missouri, Kansas, Oklahoma (Avery's home state), the Texas Panhandle, New Mexico, Arizona and then California, instead of the favored northern route through Colorado, Utah and Nevada. Originally US 60, it became US 66 in November, 1926 and was completely paved by 1935. It has been immortalized in novels, songs, a TV series and Route 66 Magazine.

It was more than just a highway, it was an American icon. Route 66 symbolized our sense of adventure on the open road and it was fascinating to travel, with its funky motels such as the Blue Swallow in Tucumcari, NM (open since 1942), gas stations, and café's like the Club Café in Santa Rosa, NM – "2 million sourdough biscuits since 1935." It also featured the Devil's Rope Museum in McLean, TX (a "tribute to barbed wire") and advertising gimmicks that include the 20-foot high fiberglass Gemini Giant for the Launching Pad Café in Wilmington, IL and the 80-foot long Blue Whale at a swimming hole in Catoosa, OK. You can stop at Funks Grove in Illinois to buy maple syrup and see the Round Barn in Arcadia, OK. The Cadillac Ranch west of Amarillo has ten brightly-painted Caddies buried head-first into the ground and in Holbrook, AZ you can stay overnight in a cement teepee at the Wigwam Motel – need we say more?! These roadside fixtures varied from the charming to the bizarre, but they all were there to lure drivers during Route 66's heyday. Many still exist along the former route. Imagine yourself driving along the highway and you feel the need to eat or have a cold drink (perhaps in the 300-mile desert stretch through Arizona and California), gas up your car or stay somewhere for the night. The hundreds of colorful businesses along Route 66 were an early American marketing machine intended to get people out of their cars, capturing their attention with all manner of signs and contraptions. This was the glory and the spectacle of Route 66 – a uniquely American experience that fed and sustained us in the days when jet planes, Interstates and 100-mph cars didn't exist. All we had was a roadster, a car full of kids and our imaginings of what magic lay ahead somewhere between Chicago and the Santa Monica Pier in California.

Kansas – America's heartland,

the Sunflower State;

time-honored values

that made our nation great.

Kansas – America's Heartland

The foundation of America is the center of the country that has been called the Heartland, the Midwest, the Great Plains, the Nation's Breadbasket. This is a vast area stretching from Ohio to Colorado and from the Canadian border to the Gulf Coast. It provides much of the grain and livestock that feeds not only Americans but also a substantial portion of the rest of the world. Kansas is the geographic center of America and it is representative of a large area that we call the Great Plains.

Kansas was admitted into the Union on January 29, 1861 as the 34th state and it fought on the side of the North in the Civil War. It is called either the Sunflower State or the Jayhawk State. The jayhawk, now the mascot for the University of Kansas, is a mythical creature that is half blue jay and half hawk. Jayhawkers were anti-slavery supporters from Kansas who raided Missouri border towns to free slaves and plunder slave owners' properties. The sunflower is native to Kansas and all parts of it were used by Native Americans who lived in the area, some for food, some for dyes, and some for the oil it provided.

Kansas is a Sioux word for "people of the south wind." Like all of the Great Plains, it was covered by ocean waters at least 50 times over millions of years, as shown by the vast limestone deposits and many types of fossils present. Kansas was a part of the Louisiana Purchase of 1803, in which the United States acquired 828,000 square miles from France for only $15 million. Kansas' history is one of exploration, conflicts, droughts and natural resources. Lewis and Clark passed through in 1804 on their way to map the West and Northwest; also, settlers' highways such as the Santa Fe and Oregon Trails passed through Kansas. Although most of the state had been deeded to the Native Americans, in the 1840s and 1850s there was a large push of settlers into Kansas and there were, inevitably, clashes. Additionally, settlers were greeted by endless prairie grasses, constant wind and a land without trees in the western part of the state, making it necessary for them to build sod huts and use limestone posts for fences (some of which are still in use). The late 1850s saw open warfare in Kansas over slavery, culminating in a state constitution banning it. In the 1860s to the 1880s railroads were built through Kansas and places such as Abilene and Dodge City became wild-west "cow towns," providing beef and hides to fuel America's westward drive. In 1871, "Wild Bill" Hickok was the U.S. Marshall in Abilene.

Kansas experiences severe droughts roughly once every 20 years; a landmark agricultural event was the introduction of drought-resistant "Turkey red" wheat by Russian immigrants in 1874. It also has hundreds of tornadoes each year over all parts of the state.

Many people only know of Kansas from L. Frank Baum's series of stories and the resulting movie, "The Wizard of Oz." Mr. Baum traveled through Kansas as an actor in the 1880s and it apparently made enough of an impression on him that he used it as the backdrop for the tale in which Dorothy and her little dog, Toto, encounter exciting adventures in the Land of Oz after her house is swept away by a Kansas tornado. In the end, it was only a dream but Dorothy's last line – "There's no place like home" – describes how many Kansans feel about their state.

The American Cowboy,

doing what he does best;

cow-puncher, cattle driver,

taming the West.

The American Cowboy

Kansas is a part of the Great Plains, where the American cowboy legend was born. In fact, Kansas served as home to many of these early-day working men in railhead towns such as Dodge City and Abilene, where cattle were driven for shipment back East. The cowboy has been romanticized in American lore through magazines, rodeos, movies, songs, novels and TV. It's interesting, then, to find that the cowboy was not uniquely American and their time in history and numbers were very limited.

In the 1700s, Spain controlled all of what is now Mexico and our Southwest. Colonization was done with missions, which were early versions of small towns. Cattle were raised by mission Indians for their leather, which was used in clothing, and for tallow (fat), used in candles and soap. Wild horses from the Spanish Conquistadors were used by *vaqueros,* or Mexican cowboys, to herd the cattle. In 1821, Mexico declared independence from Spain, ending the mission system. However, private ranchers took over cattle raising and the role of the *vaqueros* continued. By 1836, Texas had broken away from Mexico and in 1845 it became a state. American families had moved in, bringing along short-horned British cattle that bred with the wild native cattle (called *cimarrons* in Spanish, or "wild ones") to create the Texas Longhorn. The Americans learned the skills of herding, roping and branding cattle from the *vaqueros* using *la reata,* a lariat or rope originally made of rawhide. Texans changed *vaquero* to "buckaroo", then to "cowboy". To provide beef and leather for people back East, for settlers coming to the Great Plains, and for gold miners out West, cowboys herded cattle on Long Drives from ranches in Texas north to railheads in Kansas and Missouri, as well as east and south from Oregon. These drives only lasted for about 25 years, from 1860-1885, but the legend of the American cowboy had been born.

During the time of the cattle drives, there were only about 35,000 cowboys in all of the West. They were mostly Civil War veterans and adventurers from the cities in the East; one in three was either Mexican or African American (many of whom had been slaves in Texas). There were many Native American cowboys in Oklahoma. They often started in their teens, with an average age of 24 and a working life of only about ten years due to the hard riding and outdoor survival. They were "tough as nails," quiet and had a strict code of ethics. They only used guns for hunting and the wild gun battles portrayed in movies and novels are largely a myth. They would not tolerate weaklings or complainers, had deep respect for the animals they worked with and valued personal freedom in the Big Sky country above all else. They worked 10 to 14 hours a day, using three to four different horses in that time and sometimes had to work at night when storms would trigger stampedes. Cattle drives lasted for two to four months and the cowboys had to stay with the cattle at all times. For this rough work, they were paid $20-30 a month plus food. A good cook and a well-outfitted chuck wagon were important to a successful cattle drive. Trail food included beans, biscuits, bacon, meat, gravy, strong coffee and, sometimes, dried fruit. Cowboys would sing around the campfire for entertainment and also on the range to calm the cattle; trail bosses valued cowboys who could sing.

In the late 1880s, the open range and cattle drives were pushed out by farmers, fenced sheep ranches and towns and the cowboys had to find other work, which included a number of Wild West shows. Cowboys still work today on large ranches, but in addition to horses they use jeeps, radios and even helicopters to find and herd cattle. The cowboy of the Old West is still alive in our hearts and minds, though, because he represents our spirit of adventure and romance, reminding us of a time and place in our nation's history when the West was untamed and wild.

Thanksgiving Day;

celebrating our prosperity

the American way.

An American Thanksgiving In Loveland, Colorado

Farm life is alive and kicking at the Osborn Farm in Loveland, Colorado, where Dale, Pam and their three sons are the fifth and sixth generations of Osborns to work the land since 1860. At that time, William B. Osborn moved out west from Milo, New York to heal his tuberculosis and he obtained the 160-acre farm in a swap for a gold rush grubstake. He and his family arrived at the farm New Year's Day, 1861. Over the next decades William served as dentist, county judge, assessor and a number of other positions of importance before his death at the ripe old age of 91 – the high, dry Colorado weather was certainly good for his health! The current Osborns have lived on the farm since 1979, growing and selling pumpkins, Indian corn, gourds and raspberries to local customers. The Osborn Farm is a perfect setting for a traditional American Thanksgiving.

Thanksgiving is a national holiday in America, but many other cultures and countries also have harvest celebrations, among them ancient Rome, China, Israel and Bulgaria. In America, the first Thanksgiving was celebrated by the Pilgrims and a group of Native Americans. The Pilgrims had sailed from Plymouth, England on Sept. 16, 1620 to escape religious persecution at the hands of the Church of England. They sailed on the Mayflower and landed in what is now Massachusetts on December 26, calling it New Plymouth. Between the voyage and the harsh winter, only 57 of the original 102 settlers who had set sail from England were alive by spring. They met the local Native Americans, the Wampanoag, who taught them to hunt, plant corn and generally to survive. That Autumn, the Pilgrims had a three-day harvest celebration with approximately 90 Native Americans, serving wild turkey as the menu feature. They also had deer, ducks, geese and all manner of vegetables. This was the first Thanksgiving in America.

Following the Revolutionary War, President Washington honored the Constitution with an official day of thanks on November 26, 1789. From that date until the mid-1850s, many states in America had their own Thanksgiving celebrations, but they were celebrated on different days state-to-state. At that time, a magazine editor named Sarah Josepha Hale began pressing for a national holiday of thanksgiving. In 1863, President Lincoln proclaimed the last Thursday of November as a national Thanksgiving holiday; in 1939, President Roosevelt made it the third Thursday of November (to provide a longer Christmas season for businesses). This led to some confusion, so in 1941 Congress officially made the last Thursday in November the national holiday.

Since then, we have celebrated our holiday each year by viewing the Thanksgiving Day Parade from New York City, by watching professional football games featuring the Dallas Cowboys and the Detroit Lions playing other NFL teams, and by consuming large amounts of turkey, sweet potatoes, cranberries and pumpkin pie – some of it, no doubt, from the Osborn Farm. In many homes, the Thanksgiving meal is followed by a long nap in a comfortable arm chair or stretched out on the couch, with the dog at your feet and a crackling fire warming the hearth. What better way to celebrate our national holiday and give thanks for the opportunity to live in this wonderful country we call America!

America,
Las Vegas style,

where Lady Luck

often smiles.

America – Las Vegas Style

The exciting city we know today as Las Vegas actually had surprisingly humble beginnings. It means "The Meadows" in Spanish and for many centuries it was inhabited by Native Americans because of the springs and wildlife there. It was first "discovered" in 1829 along the old Spanish Trail from New Mexico to Los Angeles and later became part of the mail route from Salt Lake City to Los Angeles. The Mormons established a fort there in 1856 and permanent settlement began in 1865; it was declared a part of Nevada in 1867 by Congress.

In 1900 the railroad came and by 1905 Las Vegas was a bustling frontier town. Gambling had been legalized in 1869 and continued into the early 1900s despite national legislation against it. Hoover Dam was built in the early 1930s, requiring more than 5,000 workers and some 3.5 million cubic yards of concrete, more than the Great Pyramid. It was a benefit to Las Vegas, shielding it from the Great Depression.

In 1931, gambling, marriage and divorce laws were liberalized and Las Vegas really took off! The first casino was the El Rancho Vegas, on Highway 91 to Los Angeles, now known simply as "The Strip." Other casinos followed and in 1946 things really got weird when the reputed gangster "Bugsy" Siegel opened the Flamingo Hotel. It closed after six weeks and then re-opened with Jimmy Durante as the headliner. Three months later, Siegel was gunned down in Beverly Hills. In the '50s and '60s a struggle ensued between the Federal Government, mobsters and the Teamsters Union to control gambling and its spoils. At about the same time, several large new casinos opened, complete with something new - big stage shows. Vegas was really heating up!

Las Vegas' history is as colorful as its streets and casinos. In November, 1966, the billionaire Howard Hughes arrived at the Desert Inn, stayed several months, was asked to leave and promptly bought the hotel for $14 million! After becoming a bizarre recluse he was removed by his staff in 1970 and died in 1976. In 1980, there was a huge fire at the MGM Grand Hotel in Las Vegas and 85 people died. In addition, Atlantic City opened in New Jersey and became a major competitor to the City of Luck. It was entertainers such as Ann-Margret, Sinatra, Elvis and Wayne Newton who drew people back. In true Vegas style, it re-invented itself in the '90s with a shift to family entertainment, a transformation that changed its image from "Sin City" to "The World's Favorite Playground." Today, Las Vegas has something for everyone – art museums, world-class entertainers and stage shows, and large hotel/casinos – that literally take you around the world in a single evening. This is, truly, "the town that never sleeps." It's easy to understand why Las Vegas is one of the fastest-growing cities in America, with a population of two million people. If you should choose Las Vegas for your vacation spot, may Lady Luck be with you!

Los Angeles, America's

city of glamour and glitz; a perfect town for "puttin' on the ritz."

Los Angeles – America's City of Glamour and Glitz

Our tour of America reaches the West Coast in Los Angeles, the City of Glamour and Glitz. LA, as it is called, is a city of extremes with a backdrop of beautiful, mild weather, orange groves, sandy beaches and snow-capped mountains only a few miles away. It is one of the few places where you can surf or swim at Huntington Beach in the morning and ski on 10,000-foot Mount Baldy in the afternoon. With a diverse population and over 80 languages spoken on the streets, it may be the city of the future. The Greater Los Angeles area, stretching over 34,000 square miles and containing 16 million people, is larger than many states in the rest of America. It is said that it is "100 suburbs in search of a city," and if you drive there it seems as if it's a never-ending mix of buildings, freeways, malls and parking lots. Some of its natural beauty is offset by its dense population and the ever-present threat of earthquakes, as it sits astride the San Andreas fault line. In fact, major 'quakes occurred in 1971 and 1994, the latter one lasting a terrifying 44 seconds.

In the late 1700s, Spanish explorers and priests from Mexico built many missions – called pueblos – along the Pacific Coast, including three in what was to become the Los Angeles area – the San Gabriel, San Fernando and San Juan Capistrano missions. California was acquired from Mexico in 1848 and it became the 31st state in 1850. At that time, LA was a wild, rowdy frontier town, with frequent lynchings and shoot-outs. In 1876, a rail link with San Francisco brought some measure of civilization and in 1885 LA was connected with the Midwest; in that year, you could travel from Kansas City to LA for a fare of $1! In the early 1900s, oil was discovered in Los Angeles and in the 1930s, the rapid growth of the movie industry made it seem like a fantasy land to other Americans back east. The 1950s were a time of great prosperity when the growth of suburbs exploded and they were linked by the country's largest freeway system, which was built where electric trolley rail lines had been. Beach movies painted LA as a "fun and sun" place and young people flocked to Hollywood and Vine and Schwab's drugstore to be discovered by a movie producer. In 1999 and 2000, ghosts of the old streetcars emerged when subway lines were opened in LA to help relieve traffic congestion from automobiles.

More than anything else, LA is a city of glitz and glamour, best represented by Beverly Hills and Rodeo Drive, where you can buy a pair of socks for "only" $200! It is also home to FIDM, the Fashion Institute of Design and Merchandising. It is in the heart of LA and it is teaching future fashion and costume designers from all over the world. Tourists take bus tours along Wilshire Boulevard in hopes of seeing a movie star taking out the garbage or walking their dog. LA itself has Sunset Boulevard and the Sunset Strip, an area of trendy shops and restaurants. The LA area also boasts the La Brea Tar Pits, where prehistoric animals such as wooly mammoths and saber-tooth tigers were trapped and preserved some 40,000 years ago. LA also has a seemingly endless array of cultural attractions; there's always something to do! And we've hardly mentioned the beaches and the ocean – Venice Beach with its bizarre weightlifters and in-line skaters; Huntington and Malibu Beaches – "Surf's Up!"; Santa Monica Beach in the "Independent People's Republic of Santa Monica" with its volleyball nets, amusement park and roller coaster.

With so much to see and do, we can't capture LA's magic on just a couple of pages. If you really want to know what LA is like you have to see it for yourself. However, be careful because, as the line goes in the Eagles' famous song, "Hotel California," 'you can check out, but you'll never leave!'

Alaska,

America's wilderness **treasure**;

its **boundless beauty**

is beyond measure.

ALASKA

1919

Alaska – America's Wilderness Wonderland

Some 7,000 years ago, people from Asia crossed a land bridge into the northwest tip of North America. That land bridge is now 300 feet under water but descendants of those first pioneers, the Native Alaskans, are still living there. The land they populated is now called Alaska, which comes from the Aleut word "Alyeska," meaning "the great land." As in the days when the land bridge was above water, Alaska is inhabited by an incredible array of animals, birds, fish and plants. It is truly America's Wilderness Wonderland!

In 1741, Russian explorers, led by Vitus Bering, "discovered" Alaska and claimed it in the name of the Russian czar, Peter the First. There followed a long period of exploitation of the Native Alaskans for the fur seal trade and in 1854 Russia, needing money desperately to fund the Crimean War, offered to sell Alaska to the United States. Thirteen years later, it was purchased for $7.2 million, about two cents per acre! The Russians were delighted to have secured such a high price from William Seward, the U.S. secretary of state, who was ridiculed in cartoons and editorials for engineering "Seward's Folly," or "Seward's Icebox."

In 1880, the U.S. Census counted 33,426 people – 430 white, six black and the rest Native Alaskans. A governor, schools and court system were established in 1884 and in 1898 the Alaska Gold Rush occurred. It was the only part of America to be occupied by the Japanese in World War II. In order to bring war supplies north to combat the Japanese, the 1,519-mile-long Alaska Highway was constructed through unsurveyed wilderness in only eight months.

On January 3, 1959, Alaska became the 49th state. It is by far the largest of our states and it is bordered by both the Atlantic and Pacific oceans. It is still sparsely populated, with less than one million people. Fur trading has been replaced commercially with mining, forestry, oil drilling, fishing, farming and tourism in many forms. It has become a favorite destination for cruise ships. Many ships travel the Inside Passage, where you visit quaint frontier towns such as Skagway, walk in a real gold mine, and see first-hand Native Alaskan artifacts and totem poles. You could also sit on the deck of the ship where you will delight in viewing playful dolphins and whale pods, and you'll come within yards of icebergs and glaciers – it's truly a spectacular experience!

Alaska has been called "The Last Frontier" for its wild, colorful history and harsh living conditions and "The Land of the Midnight Sun" for its long summer days (and long winter nights). In Barrow, the northern-most town in Alaska, the sun doesn't set for 84 days around the summer solstice. The presence of whales, moose, king salmon, Kodiak brown bears and scores of other wild creatures in breathtaking natural settings of scenery seen nowhere else in America truly makes Alaska a Wilderness Wonderland!

This tropical island of sand and sea, Hawaii, America's paradise, awaits you and me.

E Nelson 2003 ©

Hawaii – America's Island Paradise

If you sail west from California, after five days and 2,400 miles a series of volcanic islands appears. It couldn't be more different from our last stop, Alaska, in almost every way. This is Hawaii, our 50th state, a tropical paradise with deep-blue waters, palm trees swaying in the trade wind breeze and flowers everywhere. It is a 132-island chain of coral and lava that spreads 1,523 miles northwest from the Big Island, Hawaii. The eight large islands in the southeast corner are the only ones inhabited and their climates range from tropical sea level to the 13,796-foot elevation Mauna Kea, an inactive volcano, where it often snows. Two others, Mauna Loa and Kilauea, are still active. Some areas get up to 400 inches of rain per year and others are deserts, receiving ten inches or less. Sea turtles and humpback whales are native to Hawaii but, curiously, this island paradise had only two native land animals – the hoary bat and the monk seal.

Hawaii is a part of Polynesia and it was originally settled by two waves of Polynesian explorers, one group from the Marquesas Islands in 300 AD and a second from Tahiti in 900 AD. The ancient Polynesians were expert navigators, sailing for thousands of miles in large canoes that could carry up to 200 people and their possessions, using the stars, clouds, ocean currents and seabirds to find their way. For hundreds of years, the Native Hawaiians lived in isolation, their daily lives governed by a set of rules called *kapu;* to break a *kapu* resulted in death. They also had several gods, including Ku (god of war), Kane (god of life), Lono (god of the harvest) and Pele (goddess of fire, believed to live in the Kilauea volcano). In 1778, James Cook and his crew "discovered" Hawaii. They then left, returned and were killed in a dispute with the islanders. In 1810, King Kamehameha consolidated his rule after a 30-year war with other Hawaiian chieftans. In the 1820s, missionaries arrived and changed the daily lives of Native Hawaiians, some for the better and some for the worse. They introduced a 12-letter alphabet, allowing Hawaiians to begin recording their history, but they also banned several popular customs, forced the Hawaiians to wear bulky, uncomfortable clothes and brought several fatal diseases that severely reduced the native population.

In 1835, the first sugar cane plantation was established and over the next 80 years or so the owners came to dominate the politics and culture of the islands. In the early 1900s, an uprising took place over unfair work conditions and control tactics and the U.S. Marines were called in to put it down. Hawaii then became a protectorate, or territory, of the United States and in 1969 it became our 50th state. Today, Hawaii has a cosmopolitan population of several million people and its economy is a prosperous mix of tourism, farming and ranching. We are truly fortunate to have this island paradise to complete the United States of America.

I Live In America,

this great land you see;
the country we love,
a nation that's free.
A past to treasure
and a future that's bright;
a beacon for immigrants
still shines in the night.
We're a good-hearted people
who want to do right,
giving hope to the world
and spreading freedom's light.

14. "I Live In America" – Epilogue

In these few paintings and historical backgrounds, we've tried to describe what it was like to come to America with little more than the clothes on your back, but with a burning desire to make a better life for yourself. This was the original idea of America and it continues today for people coming into our country. As native-born Americans, it's difficult to understand how immigrants feel when they come here. We take most of it for granted, as our lives have been privileged and blessed. However, for millions of people around the world America is still "the land of opportunity," a place where anyone can work to achieve their dreams, regardless of their background.

As immigrants have fanned out from the coastal entry points of our country, they have tended to settle in areas that reminded them of their homelands. Once they settled, they sent word back to the "old country" about the wonderful places they had found, spurring others to come here. Many immigrant Americans were sponsored by relatives and friends who had come here before them. This pattern of immigration over many years resulted in areas of America with distinct and different ethnic and racial flavors, particularly in the eastern part of the nation where settlement began. In recent years, these differences have been blurred by the mass migration of Americans around our own country but before this phenomenon, areas such as New England, the South and the Midwest had very distinct customs and dialects. Add in the movement of African Americans to the North, East and West when slavery was abolished, the introduction of thousands of Asian laborers to the West to work on the railroads, and the relatively recent influx of large numbers of Hispanics to all parts of America and you have a rich palette of different colors and nationalities not duplicated anywhere else in the world. One of the enduring successes of America is its ability to bring together all types of people and to provide them with the opportunities they need to realize their full potential. America has been called a "melting pot" and it is that – but what makes it so great is that the content of the pot is constantly changing and yet the net result keeps improving.

America is a vast country that was generally settled from east to west. It's hard to imagine that, in 1824, Daniel Webster, then a congressman from Massachusetts, said of the land on the "other" side of the Mississippi River, "What do we want with this vast and worthless area?" It had been acquired from France in the Louisiana Purchase in 1803 and at the time it doubled the size of the country. It hardly turned out to be worthless, but it is vast. Later, land taken from Mexico in 1848 spread the country to the Pacific Ocean. More recently, America has been enhanced by the additions of Alaska and Hawaii to complete the 50 states that make up the United States. Although we are, clearly, the *United* States, Americans and America foster a level of personal independence that is unique. We see it in the character of the American cowboys who settled the Wild West, but it still exists in all Americans. When we say we're "proud to be an American," we are also saying that we are proud to live in a country where we can be our own unique selves and, somehow, live in harmony with millions of others who feel and act the same.